Introduction

Table decor is such a wonderful subject for a sewing book! We all gather around the table for our most important occasions and making an effort to dress up the table shows how much we care for our family and guests. And table dressing is a great way to make our everyday meals seem like special occasions. This book has themed sets that reflect the four seasons and Christmas too. I hope you enjoy creating some of these projects for your own home. They make wonderful gifts as well!

Santa's Here! Coaster,
page 41

Fun in the Snow Place Mat,
page 20

Meet the Designer

Chris Malone has been sewing and crafting most of her life. She has had hundreds of designs published in sewing and quilting publications and has authored several books of her own. She resides in the diverse and beautiful Willamette Valley in Oregon.

Pretty Poinsettias Place Mat,
page 34

Table of Contents

*Picnic Time Casserole Carrier, **page 6***
*Picnic Time Place Mat, **page 10***

*Spring Is Leafing Out
Basket Decoration, **page 53***

*Pretty Poinsettias Table Runner, **page 30***
*Pretty Poinsettias Napkin & Napkin Ring, **page 38***

General Instructions

The common supplies, equipment and construction techniques discussed here are used throughout this book and referred to in the project construction instructions. Take a moment to become acquainted with them before you begin stitching.

Basic Sewing Supplies & Equipment
- Sewing machine
- Matching thread
- Hand-sewing needles and thimble
- Safety pins
- Straight pins and pincushion
- Seam ripper
- Removable fabric marking pens or tailor's chalk
- Measuring tools
    tape measure
    clear sewing rulers
- Pattern tracing paper or cloth
- Point turner
- Pressing equipment
    steam iron and board
    press cloths
    pressing hams/rolls (optional)
- Rotary cutter, mats and straightedges
- Scissors
    fabric shears
    paper scissors
- Seam sealant
- Serger (optional)
- Temporary fabric spray adhesive (optional)

Fabric Tips
Make the projects in this book with good quality 100 percent cotton fabric. Fabric amounts required are based on 40–42 inches of usable fabric width. Do not use selvages. They are tightly woven lengthwise edges that keep the fabric from fraying and are meant to be discarded. They will pucker and distort if used.

Fabrics should be washed and dried following the care instructions you will find on the end of the bolt when purchased. In general, cottons are washed in warm water and tumble dried on low heat.

Most patterns will indicate a straight grain line that you should use to lay out the pattern on the fabric. Fabric straight grain runs either parallel (lengthwise grain) or perpendicular (crosswise grain) to the fabric selvage. Bias is any diagonal line between the lengthwise or crosswise grain.

Press wrinkles out and straighten fabrics along at least one crosswise end to find a straight grain. Consult a complete sewing or quilting guide for tips and techniques.

Batting
The table runners and place mats in this book are made with needlepunched, polyester batting, but almost any low- to mid-loft batting will work. Needlepunched, polyester batting has a little more body than a cotton batting, does not require preshrinking, washes well and does not require dense quilting.

The smaller-dimension embellishments (such as the leaves on the Pumpkin Patch projects) added to many of the sets are made with a thin batting so they are easier to turn.

Some of the projects (such as the Picnic Time Casserole Carrier) call for a needlepunched, insulated batting to hold in the heat and protect you from hot casseroles. We suggest that this batting be used with one or two layers of cotton or wool batting for greater heat protection. Polyester can melt at higher temperatures.

All of the projects provide an opportunity to use up remnants of batting from other sewing or quilting projects.

Sewing & Finishing Seams
All projects will list the correct seam allowance width for that project. Stitch all seams right sides together unless otherwise instructed.

To trim corners, snip off the seam allowance close to, but not through, the stitches to reduce bulk (Figure 1). Use a retracted ballpoint pen, chopstick or point turner to gently push the corners out when turning.

Figure 1

Figure 2

When the instructions say to "trim batting close to the seam," cut the batting $\frac{1}{16}$–$\frac{1}{8}$ inch away from the seam. This will grade the seam, leaving less bulk in the seam (Figure 2).

Items stitched and turned right side out need the turning opening stitched closed. Fold the opening seam allowances to the inside, pin and press. Then, using one strand of matching thread, slipstitch back and forth, catching the edge of the folds to make an invisible closure (Figure 3).

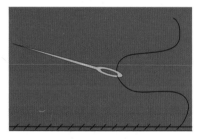

Figure 3

Appliqué Edge Finishes

When applying raw-edge fusible appliqué pieces, hand- or machine-stitch around all raw edges to secure using a zigzag, satin, blanket, buttonhole or other appliqué or quilting stitch. *Note: Without some kind of edge finish or quilting on top of the pieces, raw-edge fused shapes may eventually come off.*

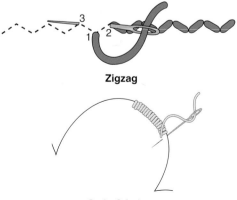

Zigzag

Satin Stitch

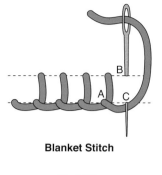

Blanket Stitch

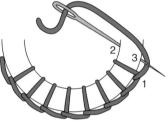

Buttonhole Stitch

Finishing Quilted Projects

Quilts are made with layers of fabric and batting referred to by quilters as the quilt sandwich. Each project will give instructions for creating the quilt sandwich and for the edge finishing technique used in that project, either turning or binding.

The quilt sandwich is basted together in preparation for quilting. You can baste with thread, pins or safety pins. Pins or safety pins are adequate for these projects because they have a minimum of quilting. If you prefer to use a long basting stitch, try not to baste where the quilting will go.

Use a walking foot on your machine when sewing on multiple layers (quilting or topstitching) to feed the layers evenly through your machine.

Turning a Quilt

This finishing technique requires the quilt sandwich to be layered with the back and top positioned right sides together on the batting. The layers are stitched together around the outside edges leaving a turning opening along one side.

After turning, press, close the opening and topstitch the outside edges. Quilt as desired or instructed.

Binding

Some of the projects are finished with an applied binding. This takes a little longer than sewing and turning, but produces a very neat and decorative edge. A bound edge is optional. Any of the projects can be stitched and turned to finish.

Cut the binding strip(s) as noted in the cutting instructions. If you need to join one or more strips together to obtain the desired length, use diagonal seams to distribute the bulk. Trim the seams to ¼ inch and press open (Figure 4).

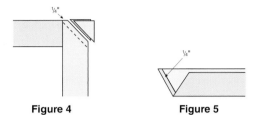

Figure 4   **Figure 5**

Cut one end of the binding strip at a 45-degree angle and fold a ¼-inch hem to the wrong side and press. Fold the entire strip in half lengthwise with wrong sides together and press (Figure 5).

Position the binding along one edge of the quilted runner or place mat, matching the raw edges of the binding and the quilted top. Begin stitching 3 inches from the binding end, using a ¼-inch seam allowance. Stitch to within ¼ inch of the first corner and diagonally to the edge of the corner (Figure 6).

Figure 6

Clip threads and remove the piece from the machine. Fold the binding up at a 45-degree angle to the seam (Figure 7) and back down even with the quilt edge, forming a pleat at the corner (Figure 8). Resume stitching down the next side, going around each corner in the same manner.

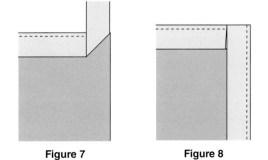

Figure 7   **Figure 8**

Stop sewing the binding a short distance from the beginning tail of binding. Trim the end tail of the binding so that it tucks inside the beginning tail at least 2 inches. Finish stitching (Figure 9).

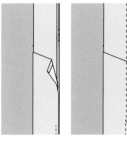

Figure 9

Turn the folded edge of the binding to the back of the runner or place mat and stitch in place by hand or machine. The corners will naturally fold into a miter; use a few hand stitches to secure the miter fold.

Making & Finishing Napkins

It's easy to make napkins in fabrics that coordinate with your table runners and place mats. There are two finishes used in the sets in this book: Double-Folded Hem and Reversible.

Doubled-Folded Hem

Press a ¼-inch hem on two opposite sides of a fabric square. Fold hem again to make a doubled hem; press and stitch in place. Repeat with the two remaining sides of the napkin to finish.

Reversible

Cut two same-size fabric squares from two coordinating fabrics. Pin squares right sides together and sew all around using a ½-inch seam allowance. Leave a 3-inch opening along one side. Trim the corners and turn right side out.

Fold the opening seam allowance to the inside and slipstitch the folded edges together to close.

Topstitch ¼ inch from the edge. ***Note:*** *To add a decorative touch to your napkin, use either matching or contrasting thread in the needle and bobbin and a decorative machine stitch.* ■

Picnic Time Casserole Carrier

This casserole carrier coordinates with the Picnic Time Place Mats and is insulated to help keep the dish hot while it's being transferred.

Finished Size
Fits a 9 x 13-inch casserole dish

Materials
- Scrap white tonal
- ¼ yard gold-with-white dots
- ⅝ yard blue-with-white star print
- 1 yard red-and-white plaid
- 1¾ yards 22-inch-wide needlepunched, insulated batting
- 3 (1½-inch) cover buttons
- ¼ yard 18-inch-wide fusible web
- Basic sewing supplies and equipment

Cutting
Prepare patterns for Flower motif included on pattern insert. Transfer all pattern markings to fabric.

From gold-with-white dots:
- Cut two 3 x 32-inch D handle strips.

From blue-with-white star print:
- Cut four 10½ x 15½-inch A rectangles for carrier side flaps—front and backing.
- Cut two 1½ x 5½-inch C1 strips for button loops.

From red-and-white plaid:
- Cut two 14½ x 35½-inch B rectangles for carrier center—front and backing.
- Cut one 1½ x 5½-inch C2 strip for button loop.

From insulated batting:
- Cut one 14½ x 35½-inch rectangle.
- Cut two 10½ x 15½-inch rectangles.

Appliqué Preparation
1. Use pattern to draw three flower and three flower center shapes on the paper side of the fusible web, leaving a small space between the shapes. Cut out, leaving a margin around each one.

2. Referring to the manufacturer's instructions, apply the flowers to the wrong side of the white tonal and the flower centers to the wrong side of the gold-with-white dots. Cut out on traced lines; remove paper backing.

Assembly
Stitch right sides together using a ¼-inch seam allowance unless otherwise specified.

1. To make the button loops, fold a C1 strip in half lengthwise wrong sides together referring to Figure 1; press. Open up and fold each long raw edge in to the crease line; press. Fold each strip in half along length again and press. Stitch close to open edge to finish one loop. Repeat to make a total of two C1 and one C2 strips.

Figure 1

2. Set the two C1 strips aside. Referring to Figure 2, fold the C2 strip in half to make a loop. With right side of one A rectangle facing up, center and baste loop on one 10½-inch side of an A rectangle with raw edges matching.

Figure 2

3. Place the A rectangle with loop right sides together with a second A rectangle and pin to a 10½ x 15½-inch rectangle of insulated batting. Sew around three sides, leaving the 10½-inch side without the loop open. Trim corners and turn right side out; press edges flat. Repeat with remaining A rectangles and batting.

4. Topstitch ¼ inch from the edge on three sewn sides. Sew three straight lines of quilting across each rectangle, parallel to open edge to complete side flaps (Figure 3).

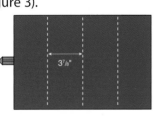

Figure 3

5. Referring to the Placement Diagram and project photo, arrange the three flowers on one B rectangle, two of them about 1¾ inches from one short end and 1½ inches from the side edges, and the remaining flower centered between and above the other two; fuse in place. Fuse a flower center to each flower.

6. Machine blanket-stitch, zigzag-stitch or satin-stitch around each flower and flower center with matching thread referring to the General Instructions.

7. Referring to Figure 4, fold the two C1 loops in half and pin to the appliquéd end of the B rectangle, 4 inches from each side; baste in place.

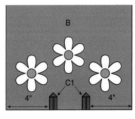

Figure 4

8. Measure and pin one quilted side flap to the center of the appliquéd B rectangle, matching raw edges; machine-baste (Figure 5). Repeat with second side flap, overlapping the flaps in the center.

Figure 5

9. Layer the second B rectangle right sides together with the appliquéd B rectangle, with the side flaps between, and pin to the 14½ x 35½-inch batting rectangle. Sew all around, leaving a 6-inch opening at the short end of B without the loops. Trim the corners and turn right side out; press edges flat.

10. Fold the opening seam allowance to the inside, press and slipstitch the folded edges of the opening together to close.

11. Referring to Figure 6, topstitch ¼ inch from the outside edges of B, and quilt by stitching across the rectangle where the blue flaps are attached and again 4 inches and 8 inches away. Stitch close to the edges of the flower motifs.

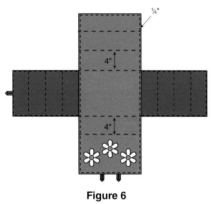

Figure 6

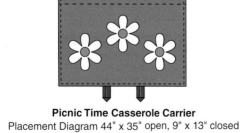

Picnic Time Casserole Carrier
Placement Diagram 44" x 35" open, 9" x 13" closed

12. To make the handles, press in a ¼-inch fold along one long side of each D strip. Fold the opposite long side over so that the raw edges just meet. Fold in half along length. Stitch close to the edge on both sides to finish (Figure 7).

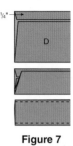

Figure 7

13. Fold the ends under 1 inch on both handles. Pin one folded end of each handle (folded and facing down) to the appliquéd side of the red center section, 2½ inches from the edges of the blue side flaps (Figure 8).

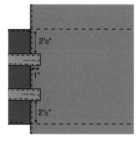

Figure 8

14. Stitch each end in place with a 1-inch reinforcing square (Figure 9).

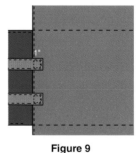

Figure 9

15. Repeat with remaining ends of straps on the opposite edge of the red center section.

16. Cover two buttons with blue-with-white star print and one button with red-and-white plaid referring to the manufacturer's instructions.

17. To position the buttons, lay a 9 x 13-inch casserole dish that will be used (with lid, if using) inside the carrier, aligning the 9-inch sides of the dish with the placement of the blue side flaps. Fold the blue side flaps over the dish, overlapping them. Place a pin at the button loop for the red button position (Figure 10).

18. Fold the red center section ends over the side flaps, overlapping ends. Place pins at button loops for position of the two blue buttons (Figure 11).

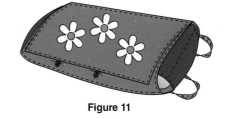

Figure 11

19. Sew buttons in place where marked by pins.

20. To use the carrier, place the dish inside, fold over the blue side flaps and hook the loop over the button. Fold the red center section over and button. Pull the handles over the top to carry. ◼

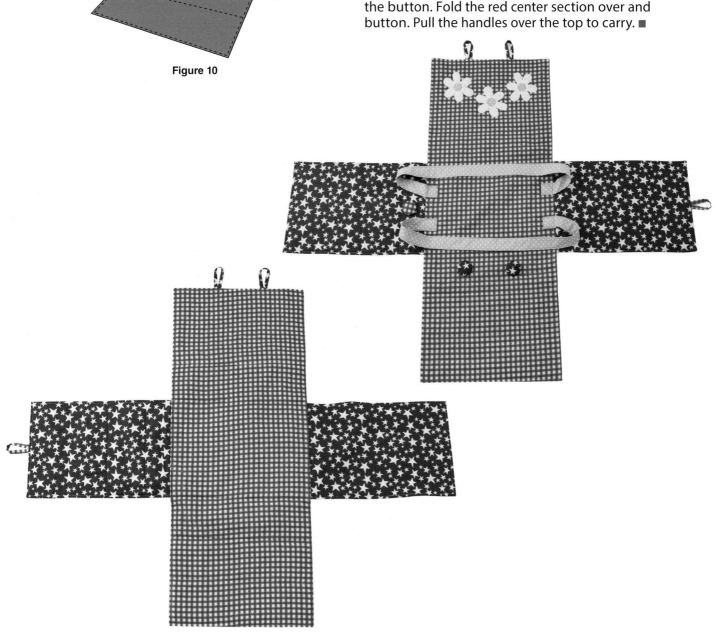

Figure 10

Picnic Time Place Mat

Summer is a great time for picnics and outdoor potlucks. This place mat has a pocket inside to hold the utensils, and it rolls up and ties for easy transporting.

Finished Size
16 x 12 inches (excluding ribbon and flower)

Project Note
Materials and instructions are given for one place mat.

Materials
- Scraps white tonal
- ¼ yard gold-with-white dots
- ½ yard blue-with-white star print
- ½ yard red-and-white plaid
- 12½ x 16½-inch batting rectangle
- Scrap thin batting at least 18 inches square
- 1 yard ⅞-inch-wide red grosgrain ribbon
- ⅞-inch-diameter cover button
- Permanent fabric adhesive
- Walking or even-feed machine presser foot
- Basic sewing supplies and equipment

Cutting
Use Petal pattern included on pattern insert. Transfer all pattern markings to fabric.

From gold-with-white dots:
- Cut two 2¼-inch by fabric width binding strips.

From blue-with-white star print:
- Cut one 12½ x 16½-inch rectangle.

From red-and-white plaid:
- Cut one 12½ x 16½-inch rectangle.
- Cut one 5 x 9½-inch pocket rectangle.

Flower Preparation
1. To make the flower, trace the petal shape six times on the wrong side of the white tonal, leaving about ⅜ inch between the shapes. Fold fabric in half with right sides together and traced petals on top.

2. Pin the marked and folded fabric to the scrap of thin batting with traced petals on top. Sew all around sides and top of petals on marked lines, leaving each petal open at bottom. Cut out ⅛ inch from the stitching lines (Figure 1).

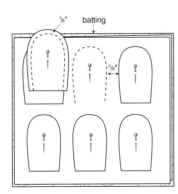

Figure 1

3. Trim batting close to the seam, clip curves and turn right side out; press edges flat.

4. Using thread to match petals and referring to Figure 2, stitch three different-length lines from the base of each petal to center and back to base, without breaking the thread referring to Figure 2 for stitching direction.

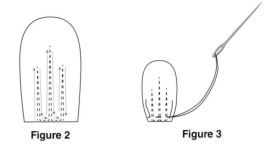

Figure 2   **Figure 3**

5. To assemble the flower, hand-gather along the bottom edge of one petal with a doubled, knotted thread (Figure 3).

6. Add a second petal to the thread and gather. Continue to add petals until all six petals are on the gathering thread. Pull thread to gather and insert needle into first petal, forming a circle of petals (Figure 4); secure thread.

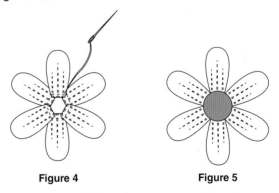

Figure 4   **Figure 5**

7. Remove shank from button assembly. Cover the button with gold-with-white dots referring to manufacturer's instructions. Glue button to the center of the flower (Figure 5).

Assembly
Stitch right sides together using a ¼-inch seam allowance unless otherwise specified.

1. To make the pocket, fold the 5 x 9½-inch rectangle in half with right sides together so it measures 5 x 4¾ inches. Sew the raw edges together on three sides, leaving a 2-inch opening on one 4¾-inch side (Figure 6).

Figure 6

and halfway up the short side opposite the pocket; stitch in place in the ditch of the binding (Figure 9). Cut a V-notch in each end of the ribbon.

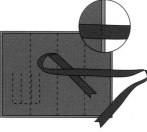

Figure 9

10. Glue or tack the flower to the ribbon, just to the left of the binding (Figure 10).

Figure 10

11. To use, place eating utensils in the pocket and roll up place mat. Wrap ribbon around the roll, and tie the ends in a bow. ■

2. Trim the corners and turn right side out; press edges flat. Fold the opening seam allowance to the inside; press and set aside.

3. Pin the 12½ x 16½-inch red and blue rectangles right sides together on top of the batting rectangle, matching all raw edges. Sew all around, leaving a 4-inch opening on one side. Trim the corners, trim batting close to the seam and turn right side out. Press edges flat.

4. Fold the opening seam allowance to the inside and slipstitch the folded edges together to close.

5. Quilt the layers by sewing vertical lines from top to bottom, spaced 4 inches apart (Figure 7).

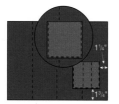

Figure 7   **Figure 8**

6. Pin the pocket 1¼ inches from the side edge and 1¾ inches from the bottom edge on the right end of the blue side of the place mat. Edgestitch the pocket sides and bottom (Figure 8).

7. Stitch two lines dividing pocket in thirds, approximately 1½ inches apart to hold silverware referring again to Figure 8.

8. Prepare binding from the 2¼-inch-wide strips of gold-with-white dots and bind edges referring to Binding in the General Instructions on page 4.

9. To attach the ribbon, lay the place mat on a flat surface with the pocket side down. Measure 14 inches from one end of the ribbon and place that section of the ribbon on the place mat, near the binding

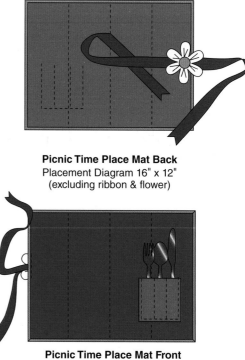

Picnic Time Place Mat Back
Placement Diagram 16" x 12"
(excluding ribbon & flower)

Picnic Time Place Mat Front
Placement Diagram 16" x 12"
(excluding ribbon & flower)

The Pumpkin Patch Table Runner

Autumn brings cooler temperatures, richer colors and lots of fun shapes to play with. String three pumpkins together and you have a wonderful table runner!

Finished Size
46¼ x 15½ inches

Materials
- 1 fat eighth brown tonal
- 1 fat quarter each medium and dark green tonals
- 1 yard orange tonal
- 3 (14 x 18-inch) rectangles batting
- 12 x 17-inch thin batting
- Basic sewing supplies and equipment

Cutting
Use patterns for Pumpkin, Stem and Leaf included on pattern insert. Transfer all pattern markings to fabric.

From orange tonal:
- Cut six pumpkin shapes using the prepared pattern.

Appliqué Preparation
1. Using the prepared leaf pattern, trace three leaf shapes on the wrong side of the dark green tonal, reversing two. Trace two leaf shapes on the wrong side of the medium green tonal.

2. Fold fabrics in half right sides together with traced shapes on top and pin to the remainder of the 12 x 17-inch thin batting rectangle. Sew all around each leaf.

3. Cut out leaf shapes ³⁄₁₆ inch from edges; trim batting close to seam and clip curves and indents (Figure 1).

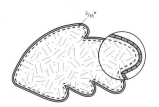

Figure 1

4. Cut a 1½-inch slash through the back layer only of each leaf shape (Figure 2); turn right side out through the slashed opening.

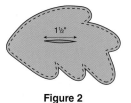

Figure 2

5. Press each leaf shape flat at edges. Whipstitch the slashed edges together (Figure 3).

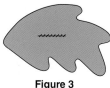

Figure 3

6. Topstitch ⅛ inch from edge of leaf all around. Stitch on the marked vein lines using matching thread, starting stitching at the bottom of the centerline following directional arrows shown on Figure 4. *Note: There will be a double stitching line on each line of the veins and one only start and stop to end the thread.*

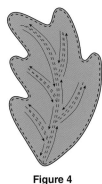

Figure 4

7. Leaving ½ inch between each stem and reversing one, trace the stem shapes onto the wrong side of the brown tonal (Figure 5).

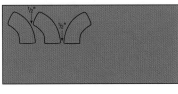

Figure 5

8. Fold the fabric in half with right sides together with drawn stems on top; pin to the 12 x 17-inch thin batting rectangle.

9. Sew on the drawn lines, leaving the bottom end open; cut out ³⁄₁₆ inch from stitched seam (Figure 6).

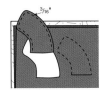

Figure 6

10. Trim batting close to seam and clip curves (Figure 7).

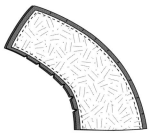

Figure 7

11. Turn right side out and press edges flat. Topstitch ¼ inch from edge using matching thread to complete the stems as shown in Figure 8.

Figure 8

12. Set all appliqué pieces aside for use as directed.

Assembly

Stitch right sides together using a ¼-inch seam allowance unless otherwise specified.

1. Select two pumpkin shapes and place right sides together matching edges. Pin these layers to one 14 x 18-inch batting rectangle. Sew all around, leaving an opening at the top where indicated on pattern. Trim batting close to seams and clip curves. Turn pumpkin right side out through the opening.

2. Fold the opening seam allowance to the inside, insert and center stem base into opening ¼ inch and whipstitch the opening closed, sewing through the stem as you stitch (Figure 9).

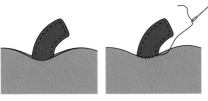

Figure 9

3. Topstitch ¼ inch from edge of pumpkin all around. Stitch on the marked topstitching lines to give dimension to the pumpkin (Figure 10).

Figure 10

4. Repeat steps 1–3 to complete a total of three pumpkin shapes, turning the stem on one pumpkin in the opposite direction (Figure 11).

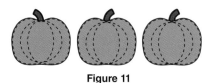

Figure 11

5. Arrange three prepared leaves on one pumpkin and one prepared leaf on each of the other two pumpkins referring to the Placement Diagram for positioning. Sew directly over the center vein stitching line to attach the leaves to the pumpkins.

6. Arrange the three pumpkins in a line with the pumpkin with three leaves in the center stem facing down and the remaining two pumpkin stems facing up referring to the Placement Diagram for positioning; overlap the edges of the center pumpkin about 2 inches on each side (Figure 12).

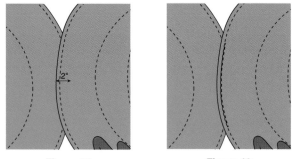

Figure 12   **Figure 13**

7. Stitch the overlapped edges together along the same line as topstitching on the edge of the top pumpkin to finish the table runner (Figure 13). ■

The Pumpkin Patch Table Runner
Placement Diagram 46¼" x 15½"

The Pumpkin Patch Place Mat

This pumpkin place mat is quick and easy to stitch up; make several for a festive fall table.

Project Note
Materials and instructions are for one place mat.

Finished Size
16¾ x 15½ inches

Materials
- 1 fat eighth each medium green and brown tonals
- ½ yard orange tonal
- 14 x 18-inch batting rectangle
- Scrap thin batting
- Basic sewing supplies and equipment

Cutting
Use patterns for Pumpkin, Stem and Leaf included on pattern insert. Transfer all pattern markings to fabric.

From orange tonal:
- Cut two pumpkin shapes using the prepared pattern.

The Pumpkin Patch Place Mat
Placement Diagram 16³/₄" x 15¹/₂"

Assembly
Stitch right sides together using a ¼-inch seam allowance unless otherwise specified.

1. Complete one each leaf, stem and pumpkin referring to Appliqué Preparation for The Pumpkin Patch Table Runner on page 13.

2. Insert stem into pumpkin and add stitching to pumpkin referring to steps 2 and 3 of the Assembly section for The Pumpkin Patch Table Runner on page 14.

3. Arrange the leaf on the place mat referring to the Placement Diagram for positioning. Stitch in place, stitching along the stitched center vein line to complete one place mat. ■

The Pumpkin Patch Napkin & Napkin Ring

Complete your Pumpkin Patch set with this whimsical napkin and napkin ring.

Project Note
Materials and instructions are for one napkin and one napkin ring.

Finished Sizes
Napkin: 17 x 17 inches
Napkin Ring: Approximately 3¾ x 3¾ inches (excudling band)

Materials
- 10-inch square orange tonal
- 3 x 6-inch strip dark green tonal
- ⅝ yard green-and-brown stripe
- Scrap thin batting
- 2½ inches ⅜-inch-wide brown grosgrain ribbon
- ⁷⁄₁₆-inch round green button
- 1 (⅜-inch) sew-on snap set
- Basic sewing supplies and equipment

Cutting
Use Small Pumpkin pattern included on pattern insert. Transfer all pattern markings to fabric.

From green-and-brown stripe:
- Cut one 18-inch square for napkin.

Assembly
Stitch right sides together using a ¼-inch seam allowance unless otherwise specified.

1. Trace one small pumpkin on the wrong side of the orange tonal square. Fold the fabric in half right sides together with the shape on top and pin to the batting scrap.

2. Sew all around the pumpkin shape, leaving a 2-inch opening at the bottom. Cut out pumpkin ⅛ inch from the seam. Trim batting close to seam and clip curves.

3. Turn right side out through the opening; press edges flat. Turn opening seam allowance to the inside and slipstitch the opening closed.

4. Topstitch ⅛ inch from the edge all around. Stitch on the marked dimensional lines.

5. Cut the 3 x 6-inch dark green tonal strip in half to make two 1½ x 6-inch strips (Figure 1).

1½" x 6"

Figure 1

6. Place the two strips right sides together and pin to the batting. Sew all around, leaving a 2-inch opening on one long edge. Trim corners and batting close to the seam (Figure 2). Turn right side out through the opening; press edges flat.

2"

Figure 2

7. Turn the opening edges to the inside and slip-stitch edges together to close. Topstitch ¼ inch from edge all around.

8. Sew the snap halves to the ends of the strip, one snap half on the inside and the opposite half on the outside so ends overlap and snap together to complete the napkin ring band (Figure 3).

Figure 3

9. Fold the grosgrain ribbon in half and pin with raw ends together at the back top center of the pumpkin with ½-inch loop extending up to resemble a stem (Figure 4).

Figure 4

10. Center the pumpkin on the napkin ring band referring to Figure 5. Pin through pumpkin, ribbon stem and band.

Figure 5

11. Position and sew green button to the top center of pumpkin through all thicknesses to complete the napkin ring (Figure 6).

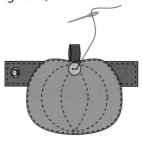

Figure 6

12. Complete a hemmed napkin referring to Making & Finishing Napkins in the General Instructions on page 3.

13. Fold the napkin in quarters and roll up. Place napkin ring around the rolled napkin and snap closed to hold for use. ■

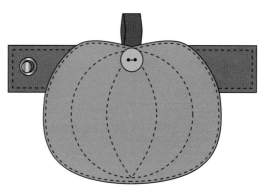

The Pumpkin Patch Napkin Ring
Placement Diagram Approximately 3³/₄" x 3³/₄"
(excluding band)

Fun in the Snow Place Mat

Complement your snowman table runner with these adorable snowman place mats.

Project Note
Materials and instructions are for one place mat.

Finished Size
14 x 17½ inches

Materials
- Scraps red-with-white dots
- 1 fat eighth each orange and pink dots
- ½ yard lime green dots
- ⅝ yard white tonal
- 15 x 18-inch rectangle batting
- 8 x 16-inch rectangle batting
- 2 (1-inch-diameter) black buttons
- 7 (½-inch-diameter) black buttons
- ½ yard 18-inch-wide fusible web
- Compass
- Basic sewing supplies and equipment

Cutting
Use Nose, Snowballs/Cheeks, Hat and Hat Brim patterns provided on pattern insert and face and yo-yo patterns made for Fun in the Snow Table Runner. Transfer all markings to fabric.

From red-with-white dots:
- Cut one yo-yo pompom using the prepared 5-inch circle pattern.

From lime green dots:
- Cut one hat piece. Set aside remaining fabric for hat brim pieces.

From white tonal:
- Cut one 14½-inch by fabric width strip.
  Subcut into two 14½ x 18-inch A rectangles.

Appliqué Preparation
1. Trace the nose, snowballs/cheeks and hat shapes onto the paper side of the fusible web as directed on patterns for number to cut.

2. Cut out shapes, leaving a margin around each one.

3. Fuse the shapes to the wrong side of the fabrics as directed on patterns for color, leaving ½ inch

between pieces as needed. Cut out shapes on traced lines; remove paper backing. Set aside.

Assembly
Stitch right sides together using a ¼-inch seam allowance unless otherwise specified.

1. Use snowman face pattern to round off corners on one short end of each A rectangle (Figure 1).

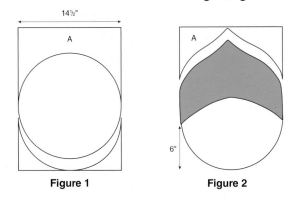

Figure 1   **Figure 2**

2. Place hat appliqué on snowman's face so tip of hat is at top of A, with side points about 6 inches up from bottom of face (Figure 2).

3. Fuse hat in place. Trim A to match the top of the hat.

4. Fuse the nose in place on each A piece with bottom of nose 6 inches from bottom and side edges of A and cheeks 2¾ inches apart and 3 inches from bottom edge (Figure 3).

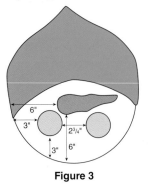

Figure 3

5. Using thread to match fabrics and a machine buttonhole, zigzag or satin stitch, sew around each fused shape referring to the General Instructions.

6. Layer batting, remaining A rectangle (right side up) and appliquéd top (right side down) and pin. Sew all around, following lines of appliquéd hat at top edge; leave a 3-inch opening on one side. Cut out batting and backing to match hat outline. Trim batting close to seam and clip curves. Turn right side out through opening. Press edges flat.

7. Fold opening seam allowance to the inside and slipstitch the folded edges together to close.

8. Follow steps 7–14 in the Assembly section for the Fun in the Snow Table Runner Instructions on page 24 to quilt the place mat, to make and attach one hat brim, and to add buttons to face and yo-yo pompom to hat to finish. ■

Fun in the Snow Place Mat
Placement Diagram 14" x 17½"

Seasonal Table Toppers

Finished Size
52 x 14 inches

Materials
- Scrap red-with-white dots
- 1 fat eighth each orange and pink dots
- ½ yard white tonal
- ⅝ yard blue-with-white dots
- ⅞ yard lime green dots
- 14½ x 52½-inch rectangle backing fabric
- 14½ x 52½-inch rectangle batting
- 16-inch square batting
- All-purpose thread to match fabrics and buttons
- 4 (1-inch) black buttons
- 14 (½-inch) black buttons
- 1 yard 18-inch-wide fusible web
- Compass
- Basic sewing supplies and equipment

Cutting
Use Nose, Snowballs/Cheeks, Hat and Hat Brim patterns provided on pattern insert. Transfer all markings to fabric.

Use a compass to draw a 14½-inch-diameter circle for snowman face pattern and a 5-inch-diameter circle for the yo-yo pompom pattern from pattern tracing paper or cloth.

From scrap red-with-white dots:
- Cut 2 yo-yo pompoms using the prepared 5-inch circle pattern.

From white tonal:
- Cut one 12½-inch by fabric width strip. Subcut into two 12½ x 14½-inch B rectangles.

From blue-with-white dots:
- Cut one 14½-inch by fabric width strip. Subcut into one 14½ x 28½-inch A rectangle.

Fun in the Snow Table Runner

This smiling snowman runner will brighten your winter table.

From lime green dots:
- Cut two hat shapes. Set aside remaining fabric for hat brim pieces.

Appliqué Preparation
1. Trace the nose, snowballs/cheeks and hat shapes onto the paper side of the fusible web as directed on patterns for number to cut.

2. Cut out shapes, leaving a margin around each one.

3. Fuse the shapes to the wrong side of the fabrics as directed on patterns for color, leaving ½ inch between pieces as needed. Cut out shapes on traced lines and remove paper backing. Set aside.

4. To make the hat brims, use the pattern to draw two brim shapes on the wrong side of the lime green dots. Fold the fabric in half with right sides together with drawn brim shapes on top; pin to scrap of batting. Sew all around each brim, leaving a 3-inch opening along one long edge. Cut out brims ¼ inch from stitched seam. Trim the corners and trim batting close to the seam. Clip the curves and turn right side out through the opening.

5. Fold opening seam allowance to the inside of each brim and slipstitch edges together to close.

6. Topstitch all around each brim ¼ inch from the edge. Set aside.

Assembly
Stitch right sides together using a ¼-inch seam allowance unless otherwise specified.

1. Sew a B rectangle to each short end of the A rectangle (Figure 1); press seams open.

Figure 1

2. Pin the 14½-inch snowman face pattern to one B end of the stitched runner; cut out fabric at bottom end to match pattern (Figure 2). Repeat on the opposite B end.

Figure 2

3. Place one hat appliqué on one B snowman face with the center bottom of the hat 12¼ inches from the bottom edge of B and sides even with side edges of A (Figure 3); fuse in place. Repeat on opposite end with remaining hat shape.

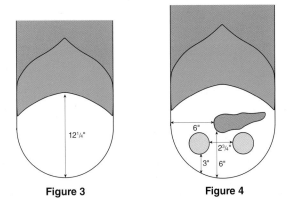

Figure 3   **Figure 4**

4. Fuse the nose in place on each B piece with bottom of nose 6 inches from bottom and side edges of face and cheeks 2¾ inches apart and 3 inches from bottom edge (Figure 4).

5. Arrange and fuse the eight snowballs to the A section of the runner, placing three on each long side about 1 inch from edge and evenly spaced and two in the center, evenly spaced between the outer snowballs (Figure 5).

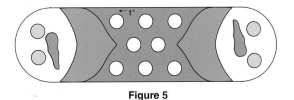

Figure 5

6. Using thread to match fabrics and a machine buttonhole, zigzag or satin stitch, sew around each fused shape referring to the General Instructions.

7. Layer batting, backing (right side up) and appliquéd top (right side down) and pin. Sew all around, leaving a 6-inch opening along one blue edge. Trim the batting and backing at each end to match the rounded edge of the top. Trim the batting close to the seam and clip the curves. Turn runner right side out through the opening; press edges flat.

8. Fold opening seam allowance to the inside and slipstitch the folded edges together to close.

9. Stitch around each appliqué shape and topstitch ¼ inch from the outer edge, using matching threads.

10. Arrange and pin a prepared hat brim at the base of each hat. *Note: Brim will extend over the side edges.*

11. To attach the brim, sew directly on the topstitching lines, except where they extend over the edge.

12. Referring to the Placement Diagram and project photo, sew two 1-inch black buttons to each face for eyes. Arrange seven ½-inch black buttons in a curved smile on each face and sew in place.

13. To make the yo-yo hat trim, finger-press a ⅛-inch hem around the outer edge of a fabric circle and sew hand-gathering stitches close to the fold. Pull the thread to draw up the edges into a tight circle; knot thread to secure to make yo-yo for hat pompom (Figure 6). Repeat to make a second yo-yo.

Figure 6

14. Tack a yo-yo to the tip of each hat to finish. ∎

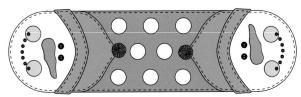

Fun in the Snow Table Runner
Placement Diagram 52" x 14"

Fun in the Snow Mitten Coaster

Warm any cold winter day with this cute mitten coaster. It's the perfect accessory to a cup of hot chocolate.

Project Note
Materials and instructions given are for one coaster.

Finished Size
5½ x 6¾ inches

Materials
- 1 fat quarter red-with-white dots
- 8-inch square batting
- 1 (1¼-inch) snowflake button
- Basic sewing supplies and equipment

Assembly
Stitch right sides together using a ¼-inch seam allowance unless otherwise specified.

1. Trace Mitten pattern provided on pattern insert onto the wrong side of the red-with-white dots fabric. Fold fabric in half, right sides together, with traced mitten shapes on top. Pin to batting (Figure 1).

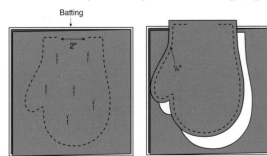

Figure 1

2. Sew all around, leaving a 2-inch opening on the straight bottom edge. Cut out ¼ inch from seam again referring to Figure 1.

3. Trim corners and clip curves; trim batting close to seam (Figure 2). Turn right side out through opening; press edges flat.

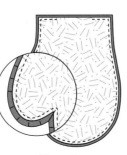

Figure 2

4. Fold opening seam allowance to the inside and slipstitch the folded edges together to close.

5. Topstitch ⅛ inch from edge all around.

6. Stitch a line 1 inch down from straight edge. Fill in that area with vertical lines of stitching, ¼ inch apart, to resemble ribbing. (Figure 3).

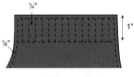

Figure 3

7. Sew the snowflake button to upper corner opposite the thumb referring to the Placement Diagram and project photo for positioning.

Fun in the Snow Coaster
Placement Diagram 5½" x 6¾"

Fun in the Snow
Napkin & Napkin Ring

Bring some color to your winter table with this napkin and napkin ring design.

Project Note
Materials and instructions are for one napkin and one napkin ring.

Finished Size
Napkin Ring: Approximately 4 x 1 inch
Napkin: 17 x 17 inches

Materials
- Scraps white tonal
- 1 fat eighth red-with-white dots
- ⅝ yard blue-with-white dots
- Scrap thin batting
- Scraps fusible web
- 1 (⅜-inch) sew-on snap set
- Permanent fabric adhesive
- Basic sewing supplies and equipment

Cutting
Use Snowball Circle pattern included on pattern insert.

From red-with-white dots:
- Cut two 1½ x 8-inch A strips.
- Cut two 1½ x 6½-inch B strips.

From blue-with-white dots:
- Cut one 18-inch square.

Appliqué Preparation
1. Trace the Snowball Circle pattern included on pattern insert onto the paper side of the fusible web.

2. Follow the manufacturer's instructions to apply the fusible web to the wrong side of the white tonal.

3. Cut out on traced line; remove paper backing.

Assembly
Stitch right sides together using a ¼-inch seam allowance unless otherwise specified.

1. Pin two A strips right sides together with the scrap of thin batting. Sew all around, leaving a 2-inch opening on one long edge; trim corners and batting close to seams (Figure 1). Turn right side out through opening; press edges flat.

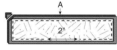

Figure 1

2. Fold opening seam allowance to the inside and slipstitch the folded edges together to close.

3. Sew snap halves to ends of the A strip, with one snap half on the inside and the opposite half on the outside so the ends overlap and snap together (Figure 2).

Figure 2

4. Repeat steps 1 and 2 with the B strips, eliminating the batting.

5. Tie a knot in the center of the B strip. Thread-tack or glue the back of the knot to the center of the A strip (Figure 3).

Figure 3

Fun in the Snow Napkin Ring
Placement Diagram 4" x 1"

6. Make a hemmed napkin using the blue-with-white dots square referring to Making & Finishing Napkins in the General Instructions on page 3.

7. Place the snowball circle shape on one corner of the hemmed napkin; fuse in place.

8. Use white thread to machine blanket-stitch, zigzag or satin-stitch all around the snowball circle to finish the napkin.

9. Fold napkin and place the napkin ring around the top quarter to use. ■

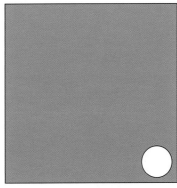

Fun in the Snow Napkin
Placement Diagram 17" x 17"

Fun in the Snow Mini Snowman Quilt

Tie this mini quilt around a basket or vase for an instant winter centerpiece.

Finished Size
6 x 5 inches

Materials
- Scraps:
    white tonal
    lime green dots
    orange dots
    red-with-white dots
- 5½ x 13-inch strip blue-with-white dots
- 7 x 8-inch rectangle thin batting
- Scraps fusible web
- 1½ yards ⅝-inch-wide white grosgrain ribbon
- Black buttons
    1 (1½-inch)
    2 (¼-inch)
    5 (⅛-inch)
- 1 (¾-inch) snowflake button
- Permanent fabric adhesive (optional)
- Small basket (model is 5½ inches high and 8½ inches in diameter)
- Basic sewing supplies and equipment

Cutting
Use Snowman Motif patterns provided in pattern insert. Transfer all markings to fabric.

From red-with-white dots:
- Cut two 1½ x 6½-inch B strips.
- Set aside remaining fabric for appliqué.

From blue-with-white dots:
- Cut two 5½ x 6½-inch A rectangles.

Appliqué Preparation
1. Using patterns given on insert, trace head, body, hat, hat brim, nose and scarf shapes onto the paper side of fusible web, leaving ½ inch between shapes.

2. Cut out shapes on traced lines and follow manufacturer's instructions to fuse to wrong side of fabrics as directed on pattern pieces for color.

3. Cut out pieces on traced lines; remove paper backing. Set aside.

Assembly

Stitch right sides together using a ¼-inch seam allowance unless otherwise specified.

1. Pin two B strips right sides together and sew all around, leaving a 2-inch opening on one long edge (Figure 1). Trim corners; turn right side out through opening.

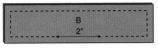

Figure 1

2. Fold in the opening seam allowance to the inside and slipstitch the folded edges together to close. Tie a knot in the center for snowman scarf knot; set aside.

3. Arrange and fuse the body shape to an A rectangle, matching the center and bottom edge of the body on one 6½-inch edge of A (Figure 2).

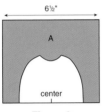

Figure 2

4. Arrange and fuse the remaining appliqué shapes to the body and A in numerical order referring to the pattern for positioning.

5. Machine blanket-stitch, buttonhole-stitch or satin-stitch around each appliqué shape in numerical order using thread to match fabric pieces.

6. Place second A rectangle right sides together with the appliquéd piece and pin to the batting rectangle.

7. Sew all around, leaving a 3-inch opening on one side. Trim corners and batting close to the seam. Turn right side out through the opening; press edges flat.

8. Fold opening seam allowance to inside and slipstitch the folded edges together to close.

9. Stitch close to the snowman motif and topstitch ¼ inch from the edge on the A background to quilt.

10. Thread-tack or glue the back of the scarf knot on the B strip to the appliquéd scarf at one side (Figure 3).

Figure 3

11. Referring to the Placement Diagram and project photo for positioning, sew two ¼-inch buttons to face for eyes and five ⅛-inch buttons to face in a curved smile. Sew the ½-inch button to the center front of the body.

12. Pin and stitch the top of the mini quilt onto the ribbon with 12 inches extending from the right side and 36 inches on the left (Figure 4). Sew the snowflake button to the top of the hat.

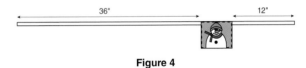

Figure 4

13. Wrap the long end of the ribbon around the basket to tie with the other end. *Note: If decoration is going to be permanent, you may wish to use dots of glue to hold the ribbon in place.* ◼

Fun in the Snow Mini Snowman Quilt
Placement Diagram 6" x 5"

Pretty Poinsettias Table Runner

This table setting shimmers with gold metallic highlights. The poinsettias on the table runner are sewn as separate petals and then attached to make them dimensional.

Project Note
All fabrics have gold metallic highlights.

Finished Size
48 x 16 inches

Materials
- ⅛ yard gold tonal
- ¼ yard medium red dot
- ¼ yard dark red print
- ⅜ yard cream dot
- ¾ yard black poinsettia print
- 24 x 56-inch backing
- 24 x 56-inch batting
- 20 x 22-inch thin batting
- Red quilting or buttonhole thread
- 5 (⅞-inch) cover buttons
- No-fray solution
- Basic sewing supplies and equipment

Cutting
Use Large and Small Petal patterns included on pattern insert.

From gold tonal:
- Cut two 1 x 40½-inch B strips.
- Cut one 1-inch by fabric width strip; subcut strip. into two 1 x 9½-inch C strips.

From cream dot:
- Cut one 8½ x 40½-inch A rectangle.

From black poinsettia print:
- Cut two 4 x 41½-inch D strips.
- Cut one 4-inch by fabric width strip; subcut strip into two 4 x 16½-inch E strips.
- Cut four 2¼-inch by fabric width binding strips.

Flower Preparation
1. To make the five dimensional poinsettias, trace 30 small petal shapes on the wrong side of the red dot and 30 large petal shapes on the wrong side of the dark red print, leaving about ⅜ inch between shapes when tracing (Figure 1).

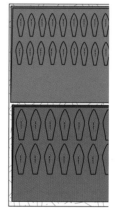

Figure 1

2. Fold the fabrics in half with right sides together and marked petal shapes on top; pin to the 20 x 22-inch piece of thin batting, placing a pin inside each petal to hold (Figure 2).

Figure 2

3. Sew on the marked lines of each traced petal shape, leaving bottom straight end unstitched and open (Figure 3).

Figure 3

4. Cut out each stitched petal shape ⅛ inch from seam. Trim the batting close to stitching to reduce bulk; clip curves (Figure 4).

Figure 4

5. Apply no-fray solution to the straight open edges and let dry.

6. Turn each petal right side out and press edges flat to make smooth curved petals.

7. Stitch three double lines on each petal referring to Figure 5 and the patterns for positioning. *Note: When stitching each line, stitch from the open edge up and then back and continue stitching the next line without cutting the thread referring to the stitching arrows shown in Figure 5.*

Figure 5

8. To make a flower, thread a needle with two strands of red quilting or buttonhole thread; knot one end. Pick up one large petal and sew two or three stitches ⅛ inch from the open bottom edge (Figure 6).

Figure 6

9. Pull the thread to gather. Pick up a second large petal and repeat (Figure 7). Continue to add large petals and gather until there are six large petals on the thread.

Figure 7

10. Insert the needle into the first large petal and pull to gather into a tight circle; knot and clip the thread (Figure 8).

Figure 8

11. Repeat steps 1–10 to make a total of five large flowers using the large petals and five small flowers using the small petals.

Assembly

Stitch right sides together using a ¼-inch seam allowance unless otherwise specified. Refer to General Instructions (page 3) for Finishing Quilted Projects.

1. Sew B strips to opposite long sides and C strips to the short ends of A; press seams toward B and C strips.

2. Repeat step 1 with D and E strips to complete the runner top, pressing seams toward D and E strips.

3. Quilt and bind the table runner.

4. Follow the manufacturer's instructions for cover buttons to make five flower centers from gold tonal scraps and cover buttons.

5. Place a small flower on top of a large flower with the small petals fitting in the spaces between the large petals (Figure 9).

Figure 9

6. Insert the shank of the covered button into the center hole; place on the right side of the quilted runner and sew button in place to secure (Figure 10). *Note: Attach thread to button shank before inserting into the flower to make starting the stitching easier.*

7. Repeat step 17 with remaining flowers, referring to the Placement Diagram. ■

Figure 10

Pretty Poinsettias Table Runner
Placement Diagram 48" x 16"

Tip

Change the fabric on this table runner and create a bright and cheery Sunflower Runner for your table. Slightly larger 1⅛-inch covered buttons create the sunflower center.

Seasonal Table Toppers

Pretty Poinsettias Place Mat

Make several shimmering gold place mats to decorate your table or buffet for holiday gatherings.

Project Notes
Materials and instructions are for one place mat. All fabrics have gold metallic highlights.

Finished Size
17 x 14 inches

Materials
- Fat quarter dark red print
- Fat quarter gold tonal
- Fat quarter cream dot
- ¾ yard black poinsettia print
- 14½ x 17½-inch batting
- Scrap thin batting
- Red quilting or buttonhole thread
- 1 (⅞-inch) cover button
- No-fray solution
- Basic sewing supplies and equipment

Cutting
Use Small Petal pattern included on pattern insert.

From gold tonal:
- Cut two 1 x 11½-inch B strips.
- Cut two 1 x 9½-inch C strips.

From cream dot:
- Cut one 8½ x 11½-inch A rectangle.

From black poinsettia print:
- Cut two 3-inch by fabric width strips.
  Subcut strips into two each 3 x 12½-inch D strips and 3 x 14½-inch E strips.
- Cut one 14½ x 17½-inch backing rectangle.

Flower Preparation
1. Trace seven small petal shapes on the wrong side of the dark red print, leaving about ⅜ inch between the petals (Figure 1).

Figure 1

2. Fold the fabric in half with right sides together and marked petal shapes on top; pin to the scrap thin batting, placing a pin inside each petal to hold (Figure 2).

Figure 2

3. Sew on the marked lines of each traced petal shape, leaving bottom straight end unstitched and open (Figure 3).

Figure 3

4. Cut out each stitched petal shape ⅛ inch from seam. Trim the batting close to stitching to reduce bulk; clip curves (Figure 4).

Figure 4

5. Apply no-fray solution to the straight open edges and let dry.

6. Turn each petal right side out and press edges flat to make smooth curved petals.

7. Stitch three double lines on each petal referring to Figure 10 and the pattern for positioning. *Note: When stitching each line, stitch from the open edge up and then back and continue stitching the next line*

without cutting the thread referring to stitching arrows shown in Figure 5.

Figure 5

8. To make a flower, thread a needle with two strands of red quilting or buttonhole thread; knot one end. Pick up one small petal and sew two or three stitches ⅛ inch from the open bottom edge (Figure 6).

Figure 6

9. Pull the thread to gather. Pick up a second petal and repeat (Figure 7). Continue to add petals and gather until there are seven Small Petals on the thread.

Figure 7

10. Insert the needle into the first Small Petal and pull to gather into a tight circle; knot and clip the thread (Figure 8).

Figure 8

Assembly

Stitch right sides together using a ¼-inch seam allowance unless otherwise specified.

1. Sew B strips to opposite long sides and C strips to the short ends of A; press seams toward B and C strips.

2. Repeat step 1 with D and E strips to complete the place mat top, pressing seams toward D and E strips.

3. Layer the batting, backing rectangle (right side up) and the place mat top (right side down); pin layers together all around (Figure 9).

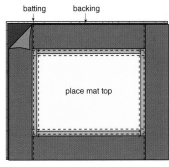

Figure 9

4. Sew all around, leaving a 4-inch opening on one side (Figure 10).

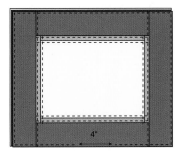

Figure 10

5. Clip corners and trim batting close to seams (Figure 11).

Figure 11

6. Turn right side out through the opening; press edges flat.

7. Fold opening seam allowance to the inside and slipstitch the folded edges together to close the opening (Figure 12).

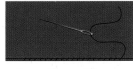

Figure 12

8. To quilt, stitch in the ditch of all seams and ⅜ inch from the outer edge. Stitch vertical and horizontal lines in place mat center 2 inches from the B/C border strips (Figure 13).

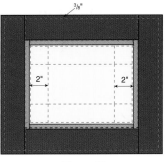

Figure 13

9. Follow the manufacturer's instructions for cover buttons to make the flower center from gold tonal scraps and cover button.

10. Insert the shank of the covered button into the center hole, place on the right side of the quilted place mat and sew button in place to secure (Figure 14). *Note: Attach thread to button shank before inserting into the flower to make starting the stitching easier.* ■

Figure 14

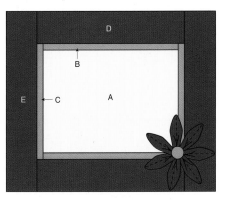

Pretty Poinsettias Place Mat
Placement Diagram 17" x 14"

Pretty Poinsettias
Napkin & Napkin Ring

Add a touch of elegance to an afternoon snack or pair these with a coordinating place mat and table runner for a complete holiday set.

Project Notes
Materials and instructions are for one napkin and one napkin ring.
All fabrics have gold metallic highlights.

Finished Size
Napkin: 17 x 17 inches
Napkin Ring: 5½ x 2 inches

Materials
• Scrap black poinsettia print
• ⅝ yard gold tonal
• ⅝ yard cream dot
• 2½ x 6-inch batting
• Red quilting or buttonhole thread
• 24 inches 1½-inch-wide gold ribbon
• 18–20 small red glass beads
• Beading needle
• Basic sewing supplies and equipment

Cutting
From scrap black poinsettia print:
• Cut two 2½ x 6-inch rectangles.

From gold tonal:
• Cut one 18-inch by fabric width strip.
   Subcut into one 18-inch napkin square.

From cream dot:
• Cut one 18-inch by fabric width strip.
   Subcut into one 18-inch napkin square.

Napkin Ring Assembly
Stitch right sides together using a ¼-inch seam allowance unless otherwise specified.

1. Cut the ribbon into two 12-inch lengths.

2. Center and sew one length to the right side of each end of one black poinsettia print rectangle (Figure 1).

Figure 1

3. Fold the ribbon ends in so they won't get caught in the seam (Figure 2).

Figure 2

4. Place the second black poinsettia print rectangle right sides together on the ribbon/rectangle layers. Pin the batting rectangle to the layers and stitch all around, leaving a 2-inch opening on one long side (Figure 3).

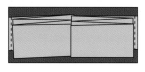

Figure 3

5. Trim batting close to seam and clip corners (Figure 4). Turn right side out through the opening; press edges flat.

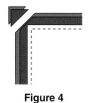

Figure 4

Using the Napkin & Napkin Ring

1. *Fold the napkin in half with the cream dots side out. Fold down one gold tonal side of the napkin to cream side at least 2½ inches (Figure A).*

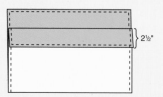

2½"

Figure A

2. *Fold the napkin in thirds and tie the napkin ring around it, tying a pretty bow with the ribbon to hold the napkin (Figure B).*

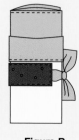

Figure B

6. Turn opening seam allowance to the inside and slipstitch the opening closed (Figure 5); press.

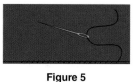

Figure 5

7. Thread the beading needle with a double strand of red quilting or buttonhole thread and sew beads to the top side of the napkin ring in a random pattern, stitching through all layers. Cut a V-notch in the end of each ribbon to finish.

Pretty Poinsettias Napkin Ring
Placement Diagram 5½" x 2"
(excluding ribbons)

Napkin Assembly

1. Refer to Making & Finishing Napkins on page 3 of the General Instructions to complete one 17-inch square reversible napkin using both 18-inch squares to make one napkin. ■

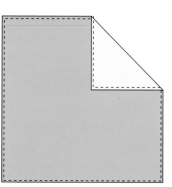

Pretty Poinsettias Napkin
Placement Diagram 17" x 17"

Santa's Here! Coaster

Protect your table from hot winter beverages with these colorful coasters.

Project Note
Materials and instructions are for one coaster.

Finished Size
6 x 6 inches

Materials
- Scrap yellow-with-white dots
- 1 fat eighth green print
- 1 fat eighth red tonal
- 6½-inch square batting
- 5-inch square fusible web
- Basic sewing supplies and equipment

Cutting
Use Star pattern included in pattern insert.

From green print:
- Cut two 1 x 5½-inch B strips.
- Cut two 1 x 6½-inch C strips.
- Cut one 6½-inch backing square.

From red tonal:
- Cut one 5½-inch A square.

Assembly
Stitch right sides together using a ¼-inch seam allowance unless otherwise specified.

1. Trace the Star pattern onto the paper side of the fusible web. Refer to the manufacturer's instructions to apply the fusible web to the wrong side of the yellow-with-white dots fabric. Cut out on traced lines; remove the paper backing.

2. Fuse the star to the center of the A square.

3. Machine blanket-stitch, zigzag-stitch or satin-stitch around the edge of star using matching thread referring to the General Instructions.

4. Sew a B strip to opposite sides of A; press seams toward B strips.

5. Sew C strips to the top and bottom of A; press seams toward C strips.

6. Layer and pin the batting, the backing square (right side up) and the appliquéd top (right side down).

7. Sew all around, leaving a 3-inch opening on one side. Trim corners and trim the batting close to the seam (Figure 1).

Figure 1

8. Turn right side out; press edges flat.

9. Fold the opening seam allowance to the inside and slipstitch the folded edges together.

10. Quilt the coaster by stitching close to the edge of the star appliqué and again about ½ inch away. Stitch in the ditch of border seams to finish. ■

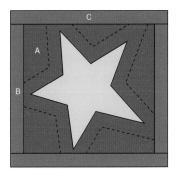

Santa's Here! Coaster
Placement Diagram 6" x 6"

Santa's Here! Table Runner

Santa's bright pink nose and whimsical hat embellishments will bring holiday spirit to your table.

Finished Size
48 x 10½ inches

Materials
- Small scrap dark pink solid
- 1 fat eighth light pink solid
- ¼ yard yellow-with-white dots
- ½ yard green print
- ⅝ yard white tonal
- ¾ yard red tonal
- 11 x 48½-inch white tonal backing rectangle
- 11 x 48½-inch batting rectangle
- 8 x 12-inch batting scrap
- Size 8 or 12 black pearl cotton
- 2 (⅞-inch-diameter) cover buttons
- 4 (½-inch-diameter) black buttons
- 2 (⅝-inch-diameter) red jingle bells
- ¼ yard 18-inch-wide fusible web
- Permanent fabric adhesive (optional)
- Basic sewing supplies and equipment

Cutting
Use Star, Face and Mustache patterns included in pattern insert. Transfer all pattern markings to fabric.

From off-white tonal:
- Cut two 2 x 11-inch B strips.

From green print:
- Cut one 11 x 24½-inch A rectangle.

From white tonal:
- Cut two 11-inch C squares.

From red tonal:
- Cut four 11¼ x 20-inch rectangles for hat.

Appliqué Preparation
1. Draw two face shapes onto the paper side of the fusible web, leaving a small space between the shapes. Referring to the manufacturer's instructions, apply the fusible web to the wrong side of the light pink solid. Cut out shapes on traced lines; remove the paper backing.

2. Trace the star shape five times on the paper side of the fusible web as in step 1. Apply the fusible web to the wrong side of the yellow-with-white dots. Cut out star shapes on traced lines; remove the paper backing.

3. To make the mustache halves, trace the mustache shape four times on the wrong side of the white tonal, reversing two shapes, and leaving about ⅝ inch between the shapes.

4. Fold the fabric in half, right sides together with the traced shapes on top and pin to the scrap of batting. Sew all around on the marked lines; cut out ⅛ inch from seam. Trim the tips and trim the batting close to the seams; clip the curves (Figure 1).

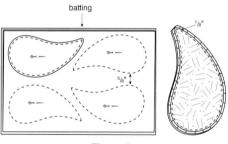

Figure 1

5. Cut a slash in through the center of each mustache shape through the back layer of fabric only (Figure 2).

Figure 2

6. Turn mustache pieces right side out through the slash; press edges flat. Whipstitch the edges of the slash closed.

7. Topstitch ⅛ inch from edges all around using white thread.

8. Transfer the swirl quilting designs given in pattern insert to A (beard) and mustache pieces. Hand-stitch running stitches on the marked lines using 1 strand black pearl cotton.

9. Set aside all prepared pieces until needed for appliqué.

Assembly

Stitch right sides together using a ¼-inch seam allowance unless otherwise specified.

1. To make the Santa hat, fold one red rectangle in half along length. Use a ruler and rotary cutter to cut from the top folded corner to the bottom open corner (Figure 3); unfold. Repeat with remaining three red rectangles.

Figure 3

2. Pin two hat pieces right sides together and sew along both diagonal edges, leaving open at bottom edge (Figure 4).

Figure 4

3. Trim the seam allowance at the tip close to stitching line and turn right side out. Topstitch ¼ inch from the seams with matching thread (Figure 5).

Figure 5

4. Repeat steps 2 and 3 with second hat set to complete a total of two hats.

5. Sew one hat to each end of the A rectangle, matching the wide edge of the hat to the short ends of A (Figure 6).

Figure 6

6. Sew a B strip to each end of the A/hat rectangle with right sides together, sandwiching the hat between the A and B pieces. Press B to the right side to form hat trim (Figure 7).

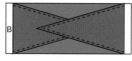

Figure 7

7. Center a face piece along one edge of each C square, matching the straight edges (Figure 8). Fuse in place.

Figure 8

8. Machine blanket-stitch, zigzag-stitch or satin-stitch around each face piece with matching thread referring to the General Instructions.

9. Sew an appliquéd C square to each end of the stitched A-B unit with the face edge touching the B hat trim (Figure 9). Press seam toward B.

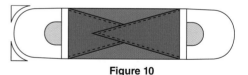

Figure 9

10. Use the rounding pattern provided on the pattern insert to round off the C corners at each end (Figure 10).

Figure 10

11. Layer and pin the batting rectangle, the white backing (right side up) and pieced top (right side down). Sew all around, leaving a 5-inch opening on one long side in the center section (Figure 11).

Figure 11

12. Trim the backing and batting edges to match the rounded-off ends of the top. Trim batting close to the seam and clip curves. Turn right side out through the opening; press edges flat.

13. Fold the opening seam allowance to the inside and slipstitch the folded edges together; press again.

14. Topstitch all around edges with matching thread (white on white section and green on center section). *Note: Lift up and pin the hat out of the way so it is not caught in the topstitching.*

15. Referring to the Placement Diagram and project photo for positioning, arrange and fuse the five star shapes on the A center section. *Note: Keep in mind that the hats will be folded down at an angle. (See steps 14 and 17.)*

16. Machine blanket-stitch, buttonhole-stitch or satin-stitch around each star shape with matching thread.

17. Fold each hat down at an angle, starting about 4 inches up from B on one side and ending with point crossing over opposite side about 1 inch up from B. Stitch directly on the topstitching line to hold the hat in place (Figure 12).

Figure 12

18. To quilt the table runner, stitch close to the edges of each star and face and in the ditch of all seams.

19. Sew two black buttons to each face for eyes, referring to pattern for placement.

20. Arrange two Mustache halves on each Face piece (Figure 13). Apply permanent fabric adhesive along stitched slash lines and press in place (or tack Mustache halves in place).

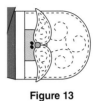

Figure 13

21. Refer to manufacturer's instructions to cover two buttons with the scrap of dark pink solid to make noses. Sew a covered-button nose between the top edges of the Mustache halves on each end.

22. Sew a red jingle bell to the tip of each hat to finish. ■

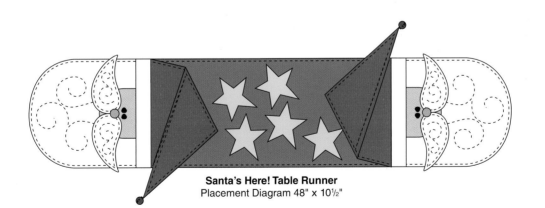

Santa's Here! Table Runner
Placement Diagram 48" x 10½"

Santa's Here!
Napkin & Napkin Ring

This adorable Santa hat napkin ring will bring a smile to everyone's face.

Project Note
Materials and instructions are for one napkin and one napkin ring.

Finished Size
Napkin: 17 x 17 inches
Napkin Holder: 3 x 3 inches

Materials
- Scrap white tonal
- 1 fat eighth red tonal
- ⅝ yard green print
- 1¼ x 8-inch strip of batting
- 1 (⅜-inch) sew-on snap set
- 2 (½-inch) yellow star buttons
- 1 (⅜-inch) red jingle bell
- Basic sewing supplies and equipment

Cutting

From off-white tonal:
- Cut two 1¼ x 8-inch strips.

From red tonal:
- Cut two 3½ x 7-inch rectangles.

From green print:
- Cut one 18-inch square for napkin.

Assembly
Stitch right sides together using a ¼-inch seam allowance unless otherwise specified.

1. Layer and pin the two off-white strips to the batting strip with right sides together. Stitch all around, leaving a 3½-inch opening at the center of one long side. Trim the corners and trim the batting close to the seam (Figure 1).

Figure 1

2. Turn right side out through the opening; press edges flat.

3. Fold opening seam allowance to the inside and press; do not stitch opening closed at this time.

4. To make the hat front, fold one red tonal rectangle in half along length and use a ruler and rotary cutter to cut from the top folded corner to the bottom open corner (Figure 2). Repeat with the second rectangle for the hat back.

Figure 2

5. Pin the two hat pieces right sides together and sew on diagonal edges, leaving bottom end open (Figure 3).

Figure 3

6. Trim the tip of the hat close to the seam allowance and turn right side out; press. Topstitch ¼ inch from the seam using matching thread (Figure 4).

Figure 4

7. Insert the bottom end of the hat ¼ inch into the opening on the stitched white strip. Hand-stitch the opening closed, catching the hat in the stitches (Figure 5).

Figure 5

8. Topstitch ⅛ inch all around edges of the off-white strip using matching thread.

9. Sew snap halves to the end of the strip, with one snap half on the inside and the opposite half on the outside so the ends overlap and snap together (Figure 6).

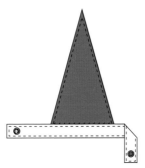

Figure 6

10. Fold the hat down at an angle about 1¼ inches up from hat trim on one side. Stitch on topstitching line to secure (Figure 7).

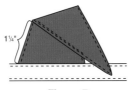

Figure 7

11. Sew the jingle bell to the tip of the hat.

12. Sew the two yellow star buttons to the front of the hat trim referring to the Placement Diagram and project photo for positioning.

13. Refer to Making & Finishing Napkins in the General Instructions on page 3 to make a double-folded hem napkin using the 18-inch green print square.

14. Fold the napkin and place napkin ring around it to use. ■

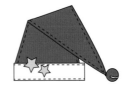

Santa's Here! Napkin Ring
Placement Diagram 3" x 3" Napkin Ring

Spring Is Leafing Out Table Runner

Springtime-color batiks create a lovely table runner that is accented with a long curvy vine and dimensional leaves.

Finished Size
54 x 12 inches

Materials
- Batik fabrics:
    Scraps of 6 or more each assorted greens
      and pinks
    ⅜ yard medium green
    ½ yard dark pink/purple
    2 yards light cream-with-pink
- 20 x 62-inch batting
- Scraps thin batting
- ½-inch-wide pressing bar
- Basic sewing supplies and equipment

Cutting

From medium green batik:
- Cut four 2¼-inch by fabric width binding strips.

From dark pink/purple batik:
- Cut enough 1½-inch-wide bias strips to make a 64-inch strip when joined with diagonal seams.

From light cream-with-pink batik:
- Cut one 12½ x 54½-inch rectangle along the length of the fabric for runner top.
- Cut one 20 x 62-inch rectangle along the length of the fabric for runner backing.

Appliqué Preparation
1. To make the dimensional leaves, use the Large Leaf pattern included on the pattern insert to trace 16 large leaf shapes onto the wrong side of the assorted green and pink batik scraps leaving about ⅜ inch between shapes when tracing (Figure 1).

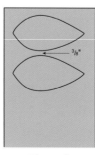

Figure 1

2. Fold the fabrics in half with right sides together and marked leaf shapes on top; pin to the scrap of thin batting, placing a pin inside each leaf to hold (Figure 2).

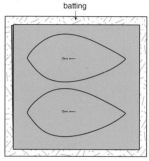

Figure 2

3. Sew on the marked lines of each traced leaf shape (Figure 3).

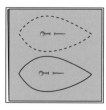

Figure 3

4. Cut out each stitched leaf shape ⅛ inch from seam. Trim the batting close to stitching to reduce bulk. Clip curves (Figure 4).

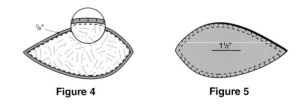

Figure 4   **Figure 5**

5. Cut a 1½-inch slash through the back layer of each Leaf shape (Figure 5); turn right side out through the slashed opening.

50

6. Press each leaf shape flat at edges. Whipstitch the slashed edges together (Figure 6).

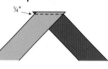

Figure 6

7. Transfer vein lines from the leaf pattern to each leaf.

Assembly

Stitch right sides together using a ¼-inch seam allowance unless otherwise specified. Refer to Finishing Quilted Projects and Binding in the General Instructions (page 3).

1. Join two dark pink/purple bias strips with a diagonal seam to distribute the bulk (Figure 7); press seam open. Continue adding strips until the pieced strip is at least 64 inches long.

Figure 7

2. Fold the bias strip in half along length with wrong sides together; stitch a scant ¼-inch seam along raw edges; trim seam to ⅛ inch (Figure 8).

Figure 8

Figure 9

3. Insert the ½-inch-wide pressing bar inside the stitched strip and roll the seam to the center (Figure 9). Press and move the bar up to the next section until the entire length is pressed to complete the bias vine strip.

4. Referring to the Placement Diagram, arrange the prepared bias vine strip in a gently curving line down the length of the runner top with top and bottom curves about 4½ inches from edges of runner (Figure 10). Trim off any excess at ends.

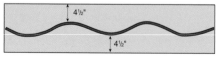

Figure 10

5. Using thread to match vine fabric and a machine buttonhole or blanket stitch, stitch the bias vine strip in place along both edges (Figure 11).

Figure 11

6. Layer, quilt and bind the table runner referring to Finishing Quilted Projects on page 4. Quilt close to both edges of the bias vine.

7. Set aside two leaves for ends. Referring to the Placement Diagram and project photo, arrange and pin the leaves evenly along the bias vine, varying the angles.

8. To attach leaves to the table runner, stitch on the marked vein lines through all layers, sewing from the base of the leaf to the tip referring to the stitching arrows shown in Figure 12.

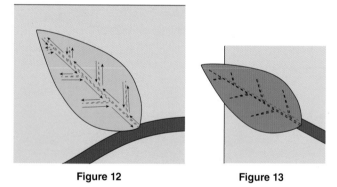

Figure 12   **Figure 13**

9. Stitch the two reserved leaves with the same vein pattern. Place one at each end of the runner and stitch over several of the vein stitching lines to attach the leaves to the runner to finish referring to the red stitching lines shown in Figure 13. ■

Spring Is Leafing Out Table Runner
Placement Diagram 54" x 12"

Spring Is Leafing Out Napkin Ring

A sweet pink flower and leaves adorn this napkin ring. Paired with a napkin of your choice, this set will help you welcome spring.

Project Note
Materials and instructions are given for one napkin ring.

Finished Size
Approximately 2 x 4¼ inches

Materials
- Batik fabrics:
  Scraps green
  Scrap light pink
  2⅜ x 9½-inch strip cream/pink
  1¾ x 10-inch strip dark pink
- Scrap thin batting
- 5½ inches ⅜-inch-wide elastic
- ⁷⁄₁₆-inch round cover button
- Permanent fabric adhesive
- Basic sewing supplies and equipment

Assembly
Stitch right sides together using a ¼-inch seam allowance unless otherwise specified.

1. Fold the 2⅜ x 9½-inch cream/pink strip in half along length with right sides together; stitch along the long open edge. Press seam open and turn right side out. Center seam on the back and press making a tube (Figure 1).

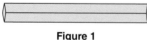

Figure 1

2. Insert the piece of elastic into the tube, gathering the tube on the elastic so the ends are even with the tube raw edges; pin to hold (Figure 2).

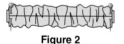

Figure 2

3. Fold the strip in half with seamed sides facing and stitch the short ends of strip and elastic together to make a circle; press seams open (Figure 3).

Figure 3

4. To make a flower, sew the short ends of the 1¾ x 10-inch dark pink strip together; press seam open. Press in half with wrong sides together (Figure 4).

Figure 4

5. Hand-sew a gathering stitch about ³⁄₁₆ inch from raw edges of the dark pink circle all around (Figure 5).

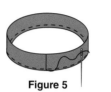 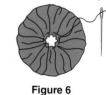

Figure 5 | **Figure 6**

6. Pull the thread to gather tightly to make a flower (Figure 6); knot and clip thread.

7. Follow manufacturer's instructions to cover the button with the light pink scrap. Apply glue to the back of the button and push the shank into the center of the flower.

8. Make two small dimensional leaves referring to steps 1–7 for the Spring Is Leafing Out Table Runner on page 50, using the Small Leaf pattern included on the pattern insert and adding stitched vein lines referring to pattern.

9. Tack or glue the flower over the seam allowance of the elastic-gathered tube; tack or glue two small leaves to one side under the flower referring to the Placement Diagram or project photo for positioning.

10. Slide rolled napkin inside the elastic ring to use. ■

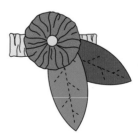

Spring Is Leafing Out Napkin Ring
Placement Diagram Approximately 2" x 4¼"

Spring Is Leafing Out Basket Decoration

Tie this decoration around a basket for an instant springtime centerpiece.

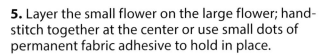

Finished Size
For 5½ x 12 x 7-inch basket

Materials
- Batik fabrics
  Scrap light pink
  Scraps 4 assorted greens
  ⅛ yard dark pink
  ¼ yard cream/pink
- Scrap thin batting
- ¾-inch round cover button
- Permanent fabric adhesive
- Basic sewing supplies and equipment

Cutting
Use Medium Leaf pattern included on pattern insert.

From dark pink batik:
- Cut one 2¼ x 10-inch strip.
- Cut one 1¾ x 10-inch strip.

From cream/pink batik:
- Cut two 2½ x 32-inch strips.

Assembly
Stitch right sides together using a ¼-inch seam allowance unless otherwise specified.

1. Join the two 2½ x 32-inch cream/pink strips on the short ends to make a 2½ x 63½-inch strip; press seam open.

2. Fold the strip in half with right sides together along length. Stitch across ends and along the long open raw edge, leaving a 2-inch opening at the center of the long edge. Trim corners and turn right side out; press edges flat.

3. Fold opening seam allowance to inside and slip-stitch opening closed.

4. Prepare a small and large flower from the 10-inch dark pink batik strips referring to steps 4–6 for Spring Is Leafing Out Napkin Ring on page 52.

Tip
To make a decoration for a different-size basket:

Measure the circumference of the basket you are using and add 10 inches. Cut two strips 2½ inches wide by this measurement. Follow Assembly steps 1–3 to make a band tie.

5. Layer the small flower on the large flower; hand-stitch together at the center or use small dots of permanent fabric adhesive to hold in place.

6. Follow manufacturer's instructions to cover the button with the light pink scrap. Apply permanent fabric adhesive to the back of the button and push the shank into the center of the layered flowers (Figure 1).

Figure 1

7. Prepare four medium leaves referring to Appliqué Preparation for the Spring Is Leafing Out Table Runner on page 48, using the Medium Leaf pattern included on the pattern insert and adding stitched vein lines referring to pattern.

8. Tack or glue the flower to the center of the long strip. Tack or glue two leaves to each side of the flower referring to the Placement Diagram or project photo for positioning.

9. Wrap the fabric strip around the basket with the flower in the center front and tie the ends in a bow at the center back to use. ■

Spring Is Leafing Out Basket Decoration
Placement Diagram 10" x 4"

Spring Is Leafing Out Hot Pad

Complete your springtime table set with this quick and easy hot pad.

Project Note
Materials and instructions are for one hot pad.

Finished Size
8 x 8 inches

Materials
- Batik fabrics:
    Scraps 2 different greens
    1 fat quarter light cream with pink
    1 fat quarter dark pink
    ⅛ yard dark pink/purple
- 2 (8-inch) batting squares
- 1 (8-inch) square needlepunched insulated batting
- 8-inch square fusible web
- Basic sewing supplies and equipment

Cutting
- Use Half-Leaf pattern included on pattern insert. Transfer all markings to fabric.

From light cream-with-pink batik:
- Cut one 8½-inch square; cut the square in half on one diagonal to make two A triangles. Set aside one triangle for another hot pad or discard.
- Cut one 8 x 8-inch backing square.

From dark pink batik:
- Cut one 8½-inch square; cut the square in half on one diagonal to make two B triangles. Set aside one triangle for another hot pad or discard.

From dark pink/purple batik:
- Cut one 2¼-inch by fabric width binding strip.

Assembly
Stitch right sides together using a ¼-inch seam allowance unless otherwise specified.

Refer to Batting and Finishing Quilted Projects in the General Instructions on page 3.

1. Trace two half-leaf shapes onto the paper side of the fusible web, reversing one.

2. Cut out shapes leaving a margin around each one.

3. Fuse the shapes to the wrong side of the two different green scraps; cut out on traced lines. Remove paper backing.

4. Fold and crease each A and B triangle to mark the center of the long diagonal edge (Figure 1).

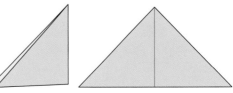

Figure 1

5. Center and fuse one half-leaf on the long diagonal edge of the A triangle matching center lines (Figure 2). Repeat with the reversed leaf on the B triangle, making sure to orient the leaf in the correct direction.

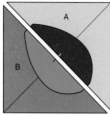

Figure 2

6. Join the A and B triangles along the diagonal edge matching edges of Half-Leaf shapes; press seam open.

7. Using thread to match fabric and a machine buttonhole or blanket stitch, stitch around the fused half-leaf shapes (Figure 3).

Figure 3

8. Center and trim pieced square to 8 x 8 inches.

9. Place backing square right side down on a flat surface; place the insulated batting square on top, shiny side down, with two other batting squares on top of it. Place the appliquéd top right side up on top of these layers; pin or baste to hold.

10. Bind edges using dark pink/purple batik binding strip.

11. Quilt by stitching close to the leaf edges all around. Stitch on the marked vein lines, stitching through the center seam and then doubling back on each stem line to finish. ■

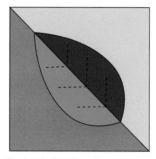

Spring Is Leafing Out Hot Pad
Placement Diagram 8" x 8"

Annie's® *Seasonal Table Toppers* is published by Annie's, 306 East Parr Road, Berne, IN 46711. Printed in USA. Copyright © 2013, 2014 Annie's. All rights reserved. This publication may not be reproduced in part or in whole without written permission from the publisher.

RETAIL STORES: If you would like to carry this pattern book or any other Annie's publications, visit AnniesWSL.com.

Every effort has been made to ensure that the instructions in this pattern book are complete and accurate. We cannot, however, take responsibility for human error, typographical mistakes or variations in individual work. Please visit AnniesCustomerCare.com to check for pattern updates.

ISBN: 978-1-59635-802-7
456789